5 Hours
A Stolen Goodbye

5 Hours: A Stolen Goodbye
Copyright © 2023 by Heather Asher

Published in the United States of America
ISBN   Paperback: 979-8-89091-099-8
ISBN   Hardback: 979-8-89091-100-1
ISBN   eBook: 979-8-89091-101-8

All rights reserved. No part of this publication may be reproduced, stored in a retrieval system or transmitted in any way by any means, electronic, mechanical, photocopy, recording or otherwise without the prior permission of the author except as provided by USA copyright law.

The opinions expressed by the author are not necessarily those of ReadersMagnet, LLC.

ReadersMagnet, LLC
10620 Treena Street, Suite 230
San Diego, California, 92131 USA
1.619. 354. 2643 | www.readersmagnet.com

Book design copyright © 2023 by ReadersMagnet, LLC. All rights reserved.

Cover design by Jhiee Oraiz
Interior design by Don De Guzman

5 Hours
A Stolen Goodbye

Heather Asher

In memory of Alani Brielle this book is dedicated to Serena Kathaleen. Gigi loves you.

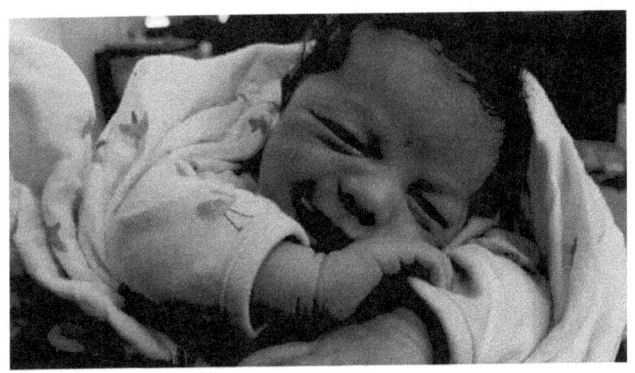

Grandparents cry twice. They cry for the grandchild they lost and they cry for the comfortless grief that their own child has to suffer.

INTRODUCTION

Hello! My name is Heather but the pieces of my heart that are my grandchildren, call me Gigi. I became a mother young and made a lot of bad decisions. Life wasn't always what I wanted for me or my children. I'll delve into this a bit further later in the book. The day I became a grandmother gave me purpose again. They all are my world. Let me take you on a journey as I tell the story of my angel, Alani. My hope is that this helps someone navigate their grief. It was a healing step in the process for me to write it.

Revelations 21:4 "He will wipe away every tear from their eyes, and death shall be no more, neither shall there be mourning, nor crying, nor pain any more, for the former things have passed away." - English Standard Version

 # CHAPTER 1

Let me tell you a story about how the most beautiful thing in a person's life turned into the most traumatic experience I've ever had. The birth of a grandchild is supposed to be joyous and filled with happy tears. My journey started out just that way. It quickly became apparent that it was taking a turn, but I didn't fathom just how life-changing it would be.

On the morning of September 6, 2022, my beautiful granddaughter graced this world with her presence. Alani Brielle was born to the youngest of my children, Erin. Alani has a two-year-old sister, Serena and a ton of family who had so many hopes for her future. Cousins who wanted her to play and all the visions of who she would become. Serena was obsessed with her sister. Every given chance she wanted to be next to her as much as possible. She absolutely loved being a big sister. Couldn't wait for the day they could play together. Looking back, I must ask myself did Serena know her days were limited with Alani? Is that why she didn't want to leave her side? I wholeheartedly believe she did. I never imagined that just eight short weeks later my life would come to a standstill.

Alani had a rough start to life. She seemed to be struggling from the moment she drew her first breath. From NICU for low oxygen to jaundice that wouldn't correct itself. Doctors didn't think it was enough to keep her and within forty-eight hours they were discharged to begin their new life as a family. Unfortunately, that life was destined to be cut short. Alani's father had decided that he didn't want to be a part of her life. Erin was alone and needed a village. As her mother I jumped right in knowing what life was like with multiple children so young. Being there for anything she needed. I'm so glad things happened the way they did because it gave me the ability to soak up all the love possible. Alani had a beautiful soul, a smile that lit up an entire room and a laugh that was so infectious.

Life after discharge turned into one doctor's appointment after another. They couldn't get Alani's bilirubin to decline, and she was admitted right back into the hospital at just nine days old. She was placed under UV lights overnight and into the next day. The hospital advised that within the last few years the levels they use to test urgency with liver function had increased. Although her numbers didn't go down as much as hoped, they felt she was ok to go home stating that although the numbers were high, they weren't considered 'dangerous'. How? How did they not think this was an urgent matter?

The nature of the issues Erin was having to navigate with Alani's health and being a single parent; it was decided that she and the kids would stay at my house. This allowed me to help tend to Serena's needs so Erin could focus on Alani a little easier. Serena needed stability and I was happy to help. During this time, we discovered that Alani was having some esophageal issues. There were no problems with eating but due to a possible narrowing, the milk was not all going down. Instead, it was dripping like a leaky faucet into her stomach leaving the majority just sitting there. She would throw up after every single feeding. This partnered with everything else, would start a domino effect of more appointments.

Erin started out breastfeeding, but the doctors advised her to stop. Stating that Alani had developed what they called 'breastfeeding jaundice'. A few different formulas later, a hypo-allergenic brand seemed to work for a little bit. Weekly appointments started with her pediatrician to ensure that she was gaining weight. In those first several weeks, Alani saw her doctor more than some adults do in their lifetime. The pediatrician would make suggestions each week to try until the next visit. If more changes were needed, they would discuss them at that time. One of those suggestions was to try a different type of formula that had already been tried. Erin switched the formula as advised and gave it a second try. Alani was seven weeks old when the pediatrician became a bit more invested and acknowledged there was a problem. She was prescribed an acid reflux medication, called Famotidine for one week to see if it helped. It didn't. It seemed that the medication made the vomiting worse. No one seemed to know what to do or how to help her and it was becoming increasingly frustrating. None of us wanted to see her in pain but what else could be done? Everything that was recommended was followed and helplessness just took over.

On October 31st Alani saw her pediatrician again. She was now just days shy of being eight weeks old. They advised Erin to stop the Famotidine immediately and to resume original formula, Nutramigen. She was provided a referral to see a gastro specialist. That would be the last time her pediatrician saw her, and she would never make it to the specialist. Alani's purpose on earth had been fulfilled but we didn't know it yet.

> *Psalm 139:16 says, "Your eyes saw my unformed body; all the days ordained for me were written in your book before one of them came to be." - New International Version*

 # CHAPTER 2

November 1st was like any normal day at my house. My daughter Emily, her husband Gabe, and my granddaughter Phoebe had just moved back from Texas and were staying with me as well. To say I had a houseful was an understatement, but I enjoyed having them all around! The adults all worked outside of the home and had gone to work for the day. The babies all went to daycare. At that time, I worked from home and waited for them all to arrive back safely. By seven o'clock everyone was home, the babies had been fed and night routines had begun. I laid down with Serena at about nine o'clock until she fell asleep. Then was able to help Erin with Alani so she could prepare for the next day.

It was about eleven o'clock when I fed Alani for the night. Burped then just held her - soaking up every minute that I could. Alani had reached that stage of wanting to look at everything. She was testing her neck strength and giving Gigi anxiety. Everything was normal. Gabe was playing video games. Emily had fallen asleep with Phoebe and Erin was packing daycare bags. None of us knew the horror that would be coming in just a few hours. By midnight Erin had taken Alani from me and went to bed. Headed to bed myself ready to do this all over again the next day. I had no clue that this sense of security I was feeling was about to be ripped from under me.

I am awakened by Erin at about four thirty crying, saying "Mommy! Alani isn't breathing!" Tried so hard to wrap my brain around what she was saying. My head was foggy, and I couldn't make any sense of it. Trying hard not to wake-up Serena I got out of bed and pulled myself together. Walked out of my room and down the hallway only to see the nightmare my life was about to become. One officer kneeling on the living room floor and heard another officer talking but not focused on him. My eyes locked on what was in front of me and there laid Alani - lifeless. The officer kneeling was preforming CPR. I heard someone comment that there was blood by her mouth. Blood? My mind started going through all the possibilities that could have caused this. Within minutes they picked her up to move outside as the ambulance was pulling up. My feet felt like they were trapped in drying concrete. It was difficult to move but I followed them out the door. As they carried a piece of my heart away from me, I was completely shattered. The responding officer handed Alani over to a paramedic. He proceeded to lay her on top of the police car to warm her up while doing chest compressions. Emergency personnel then moved her to the ambulance. My initial knee-jerk reaction was to panic…to scream.

Standing there watching everyone pass me by in slow motion. Being asked the same questions over and over. The world seemed to just stop spinning. It felt like I was watching everything from the outside. Seeing everyone close to me fall apart and knew at that very moment I had to stay strong.

> *Joshua 1:9 says, "Have I not commanded you? Be strong and courageous. Do not be afraid; do not be discouraged, for the LORD your God is with you wherever you go." - New International Version*

The ambulance sat in front of the house for what seemed like an eternity. Standing there with an officer continuing to ask the same questions over and over. The noise of everyone talking literally sounded like a bullhorn underwater. Tried to listen to what was being said around me while watching Erin. She was sitting on the concrete at the end of the driveway, broken. I wanted to just hold her and take all this pain away. Asking the officer if I can go over to her. He agreed allowing me to just simply be able to wrap my arms around her. There had been chatter about whether we would be able to follow the ambulance or have a police escort. Unfortunately, no one knew how that would be handled. Standing there all that can be seen are about six or so paramedics around Alani working on her. Minutes felt like hours. Then the head paramedic finally emerged and sat down on the ground face to face with Erin. He advised her that it had taken longer than expected to intubate Alani and they were still working hard to stabilize her. Promising that they were going to continue to perform lifesaving measures en route to the hospital. This very statement gave us a little hope that maybe she wasn't gone yet. He asked if Erin had any questions.

"Is she breathing?" that was all she said.

His response was one we didn't want to hear. "No, she isn't."

As we waited and waited for someone to tell us something, the ambulance left. Without us! Watching down the street as my heart is taken away from me wanting to scream but nothing came out. Needed to run after the ambulance. Hoped this nightmare would end. Please God wake me up! After the ambulance was out of sight, I felt nauseous and angry. I kept asking if we could leave. In what felt like forever; we were finally told we were free to go. What we didn't know at that time was Alani would ultimately end up being alone in that hospital. My heart sank but was ready to get in the car and go. No matter the outcome I just wanted to hold her. Feel her in my arms and just look at her. Gathered myself together and ran inside to grab my purse. Coming back outside an officer helped Erin up off the ground. It had taken them forever to finally figure out which hospital she was at. This miscommunication caused about a ten-minute delay. They finally got the location correct and advised us where the ambulance had taken her.

I needed Erin to go inside and soothe Serena. During all the chaos she had woken up. Before anyone noticed, she was standing in the front window watching everything. Erin was encouraged to go inside quickly. I didn't want to leave silently creating any more trauma. Erin hugged and kissed her. It didn't take but a few minutes for us to get in the car ready to leave. Our time unfortunately had already run out. A new patrol car had pulled up as we were getting into the car. The officer walked up to the driver's side and asked me to get out. I'm confused at this point, but it didn't take long for me to see what was happening. With officers coming and going the first responders were being relieved and the new shift was preparing to take over, we were blocked in completely. Freely leaving was no longer an option. We were detained without using the word 'detained'. Nobody would tell me anything except they were waiting for an update, and we couldn't leave. Officers standing in the street and by their cars talking to each other but not a single word to us. How did they think this was ok? What did they think would be accomplished by not communicating anything other than fluff to keep us on the hook and asking as few questions as possible? I started to feel like a trapped animal and there wasn't anyone there to walk us through the process. No one to tell us the next steps or simply to just be honest with us.

 # CHAPTER 3

As the first shift was about to leave the question was asked again about when we could go to the hospital. The officer advised me that it was going to be awhile.

"She just wants to see her daughter" is all that would come out of my mouth.

Hours went by and we just waited. Nothing! They continue to have small talk to keep us stationary and not ask too many questions. We deserved answers and no one wanted to give them. How could they let us go on like this when a child is involved? My mind swirled, time slowed down and nobody would say anything. Remembering only bits and pieces of every conversation. I continued to ask how much longer we would have to wait. With only vague answers being provided at this time I needed more information. The response turned to being told not that we were waiting on an update anymore but were waiting for detectives. Detectives? How did we get here? Did they think we had hurt her? We wouldn't find out that it was homicide detectives until they arrived and introduced themselves. I had also heard, don't remember from who exactly but it was said that Alani was now property of the state - as evidence! If this was true, it meant that not a single person would be able to see her much less hold her outside of law enforcement or the hospital.

Feeling completely defeated like all the air had been sucked out of my body. I really couldn't understand any of this. To make matters worse as we are still impatiently waiting for detectives to show up Erin received a text message. She just started bawling. I didn't know what was wrong. Tina, who is Gabe's mom but also like a second mother to Erin handed me the phone. The text had come from Alani's father who was apparently at the hospital.

"Erin she's gone" was all it said.

How? How was the person who didn't even want her or anyone for that matter allowed to see her? Allowed to be in the room with her? Allowed to say goodbye when we weren't? Why did he even care? I just didn't understand how this was happening! I felt as if I was in an alternate universe. Erin had given him the respect of notification about the situation even though he had never given her any ounce of respect in return. She never thought he'd have his parents drive him to the hospital much less that the police would allow him into the room. Had she known this would happen, the possibility of her notifying him would have been drastically lowered. When Erin informed him of the pregnancy, he demanded she 'take care of it' and when she refused, he disappeared. Never attended prenatal appointments. Wasn't in the room when Alani was born. He only tolerated Alani to see Serena once a week for a few hours if that. Never offered any support so it made no sense why he even went to the hospital. It made even less sense how he was allowed in where Alani was being held. I was furious inside! Absolutely couldn't understand any of it.

> *Isaiah 41:10 says, "So do not fear, I am with you; do not be dismayed, for: I am your God. I will strengthen you and help you; I will uphold you with my righteous right hand." - New International Version*

Continuing to comply but getting increasingly frustrated as to why we were still waiting. I wanted to know when the detectives would be there. I asked again and one of the officers made a joke about having 'woken them up'. Seriously? Not knowing what is going on with Alani. What was being done to her? Was the text correct and she was gone? Jokes were the last thing we needed. Completely worn down and needed someone to say something…anything! It felt like an eternity but after about four hours, detectives finally showed up. We had been trapped. Never read Miranda rights nor told we were being detained - nothing! They must not have thought we were criminals apparently. The evidence technician showed up with them as well. The lead detective handed me a consent to search for signature. This was just coverage so the technician could take the pictures. I begged them to take the formula we had been using to feed Alani to test as evidence. Alani had been born during the formula shortage and they were packaging it quickly to get inventory back on the shelves. How did anyone know whether the formula was bad? They refused. Why? Why wouldn't they want to rule everything out?

The lead detective had Erin sit down and then informed her that Alani had passed. We already had that gut feeling, but he was the one responsible for breaking the news. Confirmed our worst fear. He advised us that there had been a detective at the hospital along with the evidence technician. He offered his condolences and stated that he had a series of questions that he needed to ask. He goes on to tell her that these questions will help a panel of professionals that meet regularly to discuss SIDS (Sudden Infant Death Syndrome). So, they already had an idea that it was natural causes? Why did they have to keep us away from her? The detective that had been at the hospital showed up at the house at about this time too. I asked everyone, why someone was allowed in the room with her, but we weren't. They all looked confused. The lead detective proceeded to ask the hospital detective if he had seen anyone there. He looked me dead in my face and lied! He stated that he had not seen anyone from the family at the hospital. How did he know who I was talking about? How did he know if he hadn't in fact seen the father and his parents? Detectives had been at our house for about an hour at this point. The technician had already taken his pictures of the house/bedroom and left. As the lead detective is leaving, he again told me, "You can go to the hospital, but it won't do any good." By this time, we had been held for five hours. Five hours that we were trapped and robbed of a proper goodbye. Five hours that Alani had been alone in that hospital without anyone that loved her. Her soul needed her mommy, but it would never happen.

By nine-thirty everyone had cleared out and we were left with our own emotions. Erin couldn't bear to stay at the house nor go home to her apartment. Too many reminders of her baby that wasn't coming home. Her only other option was to be driven over to Tina's to try and rest. She was angry, sad and really didn't want to see or talk to anyone. There wasn't anything else we could do. We still didn't understand how, if they knew or even had the slightest notion it was SIDS then why couldn't we go see her? That would be a fight for later. My main concern was getting Serena dressed and dropped off at daycare. I had phone calls to make and arrangements to plan. How? How do you plan a service for an infant? It wasn't supposed to end like this. The fog lifted and my brain started working. Things that were said but more importantly what wasn't said started to fit together. Sadness took over and thought to myself that I would finally break down. This is happening…but it didn't. What did happen was more questions than answers and the need to know how this all was allowed to happen. Would we ever understand all of this?

I called the hospital to confirm whether this person had been allowed in the room with Alani. When the phone was answered the nurse knew exactly what I was referring to and transferred me to the head nurse. When she picked up the phone, the question was asked again if anyone had been allowed in the room. She confirmed that yes, he had shown up with his parents and was escorted to the back. I asked her why and how. She stated that hospital policy is that unless advised by law enforcement, anyone who presents themselves as family is allowed time to get closure. Excuse me? He could but we couldn't? Made no sense at all. At the time of his 'arrival' at the hospital, it was an open homicide investigation. How did the officer and the detective at the hospital not say anything to the hospital staff? So, do they just make up rules as they go along?

CHAPTER 4

The day wasn't done with us yet. Imagine you are just hours out from losing an innocent baby. You have waves of grief mixed with anger. Then imagine you receive a phone call that child protective services were investigating the welfare of your surviving grandchild. That very thing happened. We were informed that a case worker was on her way to interview us. First, though it's important to explain something. At five-fifteen when Alani arrived at the hospital the ambulance had given her eight rounds of Epinephrine in an attempt to start her heart. The attending physician at the hospital examined her and called time of death. She noted that in her opinion there were no signs of trauma and no foul play. So, why did they feel the need to traumatize us any further on this day? We agreed because we didn't have another choice and didn't want any additional trouble. The caseworker was informed that we were not at home. If it had to be on that day she would have to go to Tina's. We had all gathered over there in hopes of providing Erin with some support. The caseworker agreed and shortly after arrived at the house.

She interviewed Erin and I then obtained character statements from everyone else. Prior to her leaving she pulled out a large black box and advised that we all had to be drug tested. She stood outside of the open bathroom door watching everyone pee in a cup. A baby had died just hours prior, and she acted like we were going to pull clean urine out of our pockets or something. I began to feel like I was a criminal and she was a probation officer. Why? She also advised that they required a wellness check by one of their doctors. The caseworker in addition told Erin she would have to meet up to take pictures of her apartment. Even though they weren't at that location when the death occurred, she needed to see that Serena had adequate living arrangements. Erin complied with everything that was asked of her. The other parent chose not to. He avoided her phone calls and never met with her. This was the person that the hospital allowed to spend those final moments with Alani instead of us. Complete idiocy!

Ten-thirty that morning Alani had already been taken for autopsy. It would later be confirmed that she had gained her wings due to SUID (Sudden Unexpected Infant Death). SIDS apparently falls under this umbrella too, along with other causes of death. I didn't comprehend why none of the issues that Alani had while alive weren't addressed in the autopsy report. Why was there blood on her mouth? Was it the formula? Maybe the Famotidine? Narrowing of the esophagus? Why did it feel as though they had rushed her to autopsy but didn't investigate all the concerns with her health? The officers had been told numerous times about everything she was battling. Did that not get passed on to the hospital? Did they even care? It really just felt like they were trying to hide something.

The hospital wouldn't release her body until we had a funeral home secured. Luckily, I have a friend who owns a crematory/funeral home. I called him immediately. He was so sweet and willing to help me with the final arrangements. We were also faced with not being financially prepared. No one is. How does anyone financially prepare to bury a child? A referral was provided to a foundation that helps families in our situation. We provided them with all the information requested. They reached out to the funeral home and handled everything from there. That was a huge blessing! We were able to focus on the little details - dress, urn and other needs. Buying a dress so tiny for her to wear was heartbreaking. Her urn was beautiful. It was an angel kneeling next to a baby in a basket. We had the following engraved on it - "An angel wrote in the book of life my baby's date of birth, then whispered as she closed the book, too beautiful for Earth." – Unknown.

 # CHAPTER 5

It would be a full week before we would be able to see her. Exactly seven days after her passing we had to wait. We had been warned by the funeral home that they had to 'prepare' her to be viewed. She had been autopsied and embalmed so she would not look the same as we remembered her. Just to have an hour to sit with her finally was all that was needed. Her soul had gone home but we knew she would still be there with us. The funeral home had already been provided with the urn, her dress, her favorite blanket, and a satin-lined basket. All we had to do was show up.

Upon arrival at the funeral home, we had discussed that Erin would go in first by herself. She needed that alone time with Alani, no matter how long. As the family began to show up, we gathered in the lobby. Nobody really knew the words to say. What can you say at that moment? Nothing makes it better, but we tried. Everyone was anxious to see Alani but understood the necessity of Erin having that time to cry and say goodbye - alone. When the usher motioned that we were able to go in a wave of relief rushed over me. I would finally be with her again. Serena and Phoebe were with us too, which was important. They knew something was different and deserved to have closure. Letting everyone go in ahead of me, truly didn't know what my reaction would be and just needed some distance. Not at all prepared and my heart just ached. Seeing her just provided validation that her soul was with Jesus, and it was just her earthly vessel that laid there.

I sat on the step next to the basket and just looked at her. Every inch of her was inspected, at least what was allowed to be seen. Caressed her fingers with tears welling up. Sitting in silence with the tears steadily streaming down, I was able to talk to her. I told her that her mommy and sister would be ok down here. Wanted Alani to know that the village was ready to support her mom. Serena wanted to be picked up by Erin. She lifted her up into her arms. So sweetly Serena looked down where her sister was laid and said, "Bye Bye Ani". The words that came out of her mouth were so innocent. For someone so young she certainly knew. Commence the ugly cry! I think we all did. We hugged, cried, and supported each other as best as we could. Our time with Alani had come to an end. Walking out of that room was tougher than I could have ever imagined. Not wanting to leave her but reminding myself that she would be with us always.

5 HOURS: A STOLEN GOODBYE

Matthew 5:4 says, "Blessed are those who mourn, for they will be comforted." - New International Version

The following days seemed to just drag on. Lost and no idea what to do. We decided to have a memorial for Alani on December 3rd. So much had to be done and absolutely no focus. Song lists, pictures to print, and memorial cards to design. Thoughts of the next steps and what our new normal would be flooded my mind. I should mention that my daughter Emily had also announced a few months prior that she was expecting another baby. Feelings of guilt washed over me. How would these feelings be navigated? Is it possible to attach without feeling that another baby would be taken away from me? Guilt, anger, immense grief and so many others. All these feelings and no idea how to work through them. A total emotional wreck!

In the days right after Alani passed my mom had reached out to the care team at her church. People began to reach out. Meals, prayers and love. They did not know me but that didn't matter. God knew me and they were showing God's love through themselves. This was my first experience with unconditional love from complete strangers. God was trying to show me that through the storm, he was beside me. We met with the pastor to talk about plans for the memorial. Memories of Alani and who she was in her short eight weeks. Erin was mad at

God. She couldn't understand why her child had to go to heaven. She was just getting to know her and still bonding. The pastor told her it was ok to have those feelings, just don't stay in them. God would meet her exactly where she was.

During the next month I spent a lot of time researching, making phone calls, and trying to comprehend how those five hours were allowed to happen. How could no one take accountability and tell us the truth? I read Florida State Statutes as well as the policies and procedures that are taught to officers. If they had strict guidelines to follow, I wanted to know if they did or not. I felt a sense of desperation to know why. I hit roadblock after roadblock, but it didn't stop me. It was almost an addiction. When one door closed, I tried to find a window. I woke every morning thinking about who could be called, where else I could look to find the information, and wondering if the people around me were sick of hearing me talk about it yet.

The weekend of the memorial finally arrived. The enemy was doing everything in his power to put a dark cloud over our celebration. From an electrical outage, the well pump going out, a train blocking the only easy way out of the neighborhood, forgetting the urn and the frames holding Alani's pictures breaking. I arrived at the church deflated but trying to stay strong. Members of the care team had volunteered to assist with whatever was needed that day. They could see the defeat all over my face. They simply just hugged me and said it would all be ok. My family had driven in from out of town and one of my closest friends, Stefanie had driven all the way from Mississippi to be there for us. The enemy would not stop the celebration of her short little life. The service was beautiful. Pictures of Alani floated across the screen for everyone to see. The pastor told the story of Lazarus. How Jesus met Mary and Martha right where they were in their grief. It was okay to feel every emotion but to trust in the Lord as he would be there with you.

After the memorial, our whole group met for dinner at one of our favorite places. We had ordered biodegradable lanterns to send up to heaven for Alani. We fellowshipped, laughed, and honored her in the best way possible – with family. Alani was right there with us, and it was a beautiful way to end the day. As the weekend ended, life for everyone would go back to normal. I had to take a few days to just be still. Life for me was never going to be normal again. Erin and Serena had gone back home by this time, so my house was a little quieter. Almost too quiet sometimes and I was left with the hamster in my brain that just kept spinning. I knew that the need to organize my next steps was crucial to maintaining some form of sanity.

CHAPTER 6

We had filed a formal complaint with Internal Affairs within days after Alani had passed. The need for some form of an answer as to why we were treated that way. For someone to be held accountable for the trauma that was caused. About a week later Erin would receive a letter from the sheriff stating that our concerns would be investigated. Hopeful that answers would be provided, and accountability would be admitted. It didn't take long to hear back from the sheriff's office via phone call. The lieutenant had been tasked with the responsibility to advise us of the final result of the investigation. No consequences would be faced. The caller stated the events that transpired were the result of a 'training issue'. A training issue! So, they had excused being kept from the most important goodbye due to training? Lack of appropriate training left us with trauma towards law enforcement? Training issues left us with a gaping hole in our hearts that would never fully heal? We never received a copy of anything only a phone call. It took the news station requesting a copy of the investigative report for us to see it. Shouldn't they have sent it to us? Did they think we were just going to give up on getting answers?

I turned my grief around and used it. Finding out why this all happened turned into even more of a mission. No family should ever have to experience what we went through. Wanting the sheriff's office to know not only were we mistreated but they needed change in their system. So, my own investigation continued. Requested reports, body cam footage, dispatch records and called the local news station. The need to bring attention to the situation and for our story to be heard was a priority. We couldn't be the only family this happened to. Our story could help someone. The decision was made to fight for change.

My search revealed that during our 'detainment', one officer was told to 'stall' us. Our rights were trampled on, and we were STALLED? Never read our Miranda Rights. Never advised we were being detained and now I knew why. They must not have considered us a threat or felt too strongly that we had done something wrong. It was also discovered that the first shift that had responded didn't have a supervisor on the scene. So, what I was hearing was that I had a bunch of rouge officers hyped up because there was a baby involved and they didn't follow protocol? They traumatized us! I had always been under the impression it was innocent until proven guilty not the other way around. Apparently, that is a wrong assumption! It was also uncovered that the sheriff's office had violated one of their own policies when they allowed an unauthorized person, during an open homicide investigation in with evidence. Really? We were 'stalled' for hours but someone can just walk right into the hospital and be granted access? Accountability was non-existent. This discovery fueled my desire and validated that I was on the right track. In the hopes that someone would listen a full case review was requested. Just because they are law enforcement doesn't mean that they are above liability, right? They are human. So why are there not watchmen monitoring them? Change was necessary and I became determined to fight for it.

February 2nd of 2023 came, and we were sitting down telling our story to the local news. They listened with compassion, and it seemed like they really wanted to help get our story out. We had all the documents, footage, and pictures handed to them over the course of the next few months. Countless phone calls, records requests, and my own research. The emotions of reliving those five long hours brought me back to standing in the living room every time. It felt like forever as we waited for everything to be put together and the story to be aired. I learned a lot about patience during this process. It was hard but still told the story to everyone possible. Even found myself reaching out to find an attorney to hold them accountable. Not a single attorney felt that they could win against the big bad sheriff's office. Why?

There's that 'too big to touch' mentality that they have gotten away with for so long.

On April 27th, I received a text from the news station advising the story was ready to air. Did a lot of praying after that notification. Prayed that the reception would be positive, and that the hate would be minimal. In addition, I prayed for strength. Emily had come home with the new baby, Penelope on that very same day. Reliving the trauma for the world to see and having a new baby in the house again. Terrified was an understatement. This was next level! As I watched the story online the tears flowed. Scared to get attached to this precious newborn that was now in the house. Sleep was already hard to come by. When Serena was at the house, I consistently checked to ensure she was still breathing. This was so extremely hard to navigate. The response was exactly what I prayed for though. Caring, concern, and the demand for accountability. People were finally seeing how the events had played out.

I found God through all of this. Finally realized that I couldn't do life by myself and accepted that it wasn't meant to be done alone. As alluded to at the beginning of this journey, life had been a struggle for many years. That timeframe was a blur. Selfishness, manipulation, and survival mode. Took myself into some of the deepest darkest pits ever seen. I always knew who my Lord and Savior was but refused to accept his grace and mercy in my life. I was going to do things my way. That didn't work. Losing Alani changed my life forever. Decided it was time to stop running. I jumped headfirst into the Word and made the conscious decision to allow Christ into my life. Accepting that I was the one he left the ninety-nine for. I was home. Feeling a peace that surpassed my understanding I made the decision to join the very church that had surrounded me with love.

CHAPTER 7

We finally got a meeting with the sheriff's office to go over the case. Felt very hopeful for answers. Sitting at a table with the Assistant Chief of Investigations, Sergeant, Lieutenant, Homicide Detective, and a Victim's Advocate. We were sure this was going to be a good thing. Every single time I get my hopes up though they are shattered. Our voices didn't matter, and our concerns were unwarranted. We were again told that the events could've been handled differently, and that additional training was being worked on. Stated that whether we believed it or not, we had been handled with compassion. Assuring us that no major policies were violated and the 'mishap' at the hospital had been addressed. Still no consequences for any officers though. The question was asked about specific policies regarding how officers are trained to handle infant/child death investigations. The answer provided was shocking!

"We don't have specific training for that. Every infant/child death (with some exceptions) is treated as a homicide and investigated as such."

So guilty until proven innocent is the standard apparently. Not every parent hurts their child, but the first response is to assume that they do. Almost every single concern we had was dismissed. Nothing was accomplished and still had more questions than answers. Left that meeting feeling even more confident I was on the right path and there was a message to be heard.

We had been contacted by a local advocacy group after our first story aired. Our voices were being heard just not by the people we wanted to listen. I decided that this was a start and exactly what we needed. Getting the public involved and bringing awareness to a topic that nobody really wants to talk about was very necessary. A public community vigil was held, and all news outlets had been invited. Never attended a vigil much less organized one. I relied heavily on the advice of the group. Could not have asked for a more perfect event. Members of the community showed up for the cause. People who didn't know us showed their support because what's wrong is wrong. It was amazing to see people come together for the greater cause. Mothers who were in the same situation spoke out. We honored Alani and peacefully got the message out. Our journey is far from over though. At what point do more people stand up and demand accountability? Change is needed!

We have specific changes that we want to see happen and will continue to advocate for. Officers are trained for certain things, but they are not fully trained to deal with a grieving family who has just found their child unresponsive. There needs to be specific training regarding infant/child death investigations from an outside accredited source. I don't feel that homicide detectives should be training from the inside, it should be a neutral party providing that. Uniform policy changes regarding infant/child death investigations. If they are going to say that almost all cases are treated the same way but make up their own rules at the moment that isn't fair. Policies need to be across the board and handled the same way every time. Civilian oversight of investigations. When I asked who was watching the watchmen this is what I was referring to. Why is there no one quality checking? Is this how they have been able to do whatever they want because they have no one to answer to? Designated advocates for the families during these horrific circumstances. If the officers and detectives are focused on finding out what has happened to the child who is there for the family? Who is there to walk them through what is going to happen and why? Unfortunately, it took losing Alani for my eyes to be opened on how people in this position are treated. I have always had respect for law enforcement but now I can't drive down the road without being scared. Worried that because of the 'trouble' I am causing that they will retaliate. Worried for my family because we are standing up for what is right. I will stand in my faith and trust that God knows how this story ends. HIS will be done, not mine. Continue to pray for guidance and validation I'm making the right decisions for HIS glory - not mine.

Isaiah 40:31 says, "but those who hope in the LORD will renew their strength. They will soar on wings likes eagles; they will run and not grow weary; they will walk and not be faint." - New International Version

My prayer for anyone reading this is for you to know you aren't alone. That you find strength and peace in the arms of God. Storms may come but rest assured God is with you. This was a club I never thought I'd be a part of, but there is strength in numbers. Love each other and never take a single day for granted. None of us are immune to grief. Death is a natural part of life but when it takes a child it's a different kind of pain. I am praying for every one of you even without knowing you. You matter and your feelings matter. Always trust your intuition when something doesn't feel right. I love you all and I ask that you love each other. This life is a journey and one that we aren't equipped to do alone. Lean on one another and give yourselves grace. There is no manual on how to grieve so be patient with yourself.

A PRAYER FOR COMFORT

Jesus, my pain is so deep, my anger is fierce, and my fear is debilitating. In the middle of all these emotions, numbness sets in. I struggle to find the words to pray. I know you are meeting me right where I am in my grief. I know you are mending the brokenness even when I can't see it. Lord, hold me in Your arms. I humbly come to you with a heavy heart. Wipe my tears, Lord, I pray that as I go through this season of sadness you would show me Your love. I lift to you those who have lost someone close to them. Cover them and give them strength. Loss is painful but child loss is beyond comprehension. Grief consumes us. Give us Your peace to catch our breath. Hold us in the comfort of Your wings. In Jesus' name, Amen.

www.ingramcontent.com/pod-product-compliance
Lightning Source LLC
LaVergne TN
LVHW010416070526
838199LV00064B/5317